CENGAGE Learning

Short Stories for Students, Volume 16

Project Editor: David Galens

Editorial: Anne Marie Hacht, Michelle Kazensky, Michael L. LaBlanc, Ira Mark Milne, Pam Revitzer, Kathy Sauer, Timothy J. Sisler, Jennifer Smith, Daniel Toronto, Carol Ullmann **Research**: Sarah Genik

Permissions: Margaret Chamberlain, Debra Freitas **Manufacturing**: Stacy Melson

Imaging and Multimedia: Lezlie Light, Kelly A. Quin, Luke Rademacher **Product Design**: Pamela A. E. Galbreath, Michael Logusz © 2002 by Gale. Gale is an imprint of The Gale Group, Inc., a division of Cengage Learning Inc.

For more information, contact
The Gale Group, Inc.

27500 Drake Rd.
Farmington Hills, Ml 48331-3535
Or you can visit our Internet site at
http://www.gale.com

ALL RIGHTS RESERVED

For permission to use material from this product,
submit your request via Web at http://www.gale-
edit.com/permissions, or you may download our
Permissions Request form and submit your request
by fax or mail to: *Permissions Department*
The Gale Group, Inc.
27500 Drake Rd.
Farmington Hills, Ml 48331-3535
Permissions Hotline:
248-699-8006 or 800-877-4253, ext. 8006
Fax: 248-699-8074 or 800-762-4058

Since this page cannot legibly accommodate all
copyright notices, the acknowledgments constitute
an extension of the copyright notice.

While every effort has been made to ensure the
reliability of the information presented in this
publication, The Gale Group, Inc. does not
guarantee the accuracy of the data contained herein.
The Gale Group, Inc. accepts no payment for

listing; and inclusion in the publication of any organization, agency, institution, publication, service, or individual does not imply endorsement of the editors or publisher. Errors brought to the attention of the publisher and verified to the satisfaction of the publisher will be corrected in future editions.

ISBN 0-7876-4268-1
ISSN 1092-7735

Printed in the United States of America
10 9 8 7 6 5 4

Rules of the Game

Amy Tan 1989

Introduction

In 1989, Amy Tan's first book, *The Joy Luck Club*, sold 275,000 hardcover copies in its first Putnam publication, paving the way for other first-time Asian-American writers. Although Tan has since written other critically acclaimed books, such as *The Kitchen God's Wife* and *The Hundred Secret Senses*, many still feel that Tan's first effort was her most important. *The Joy Luck Club* is hailed for its discussion of both Chinese Americans and mother-daughter relationships. Set in San Francisco in the 1980s, the majority of the book is told in flashback, and is organized into sixteen separate tales, all narrated by either a Chinese-born mother or her American-born daughter. "Rules of the Game," narrated by one of the daughters, Waverly Jong, details Waverly's rise and fall as an American chess champion when she is a child.

Tan had many inspirations for writing the book. The most direct influence was her first trip to China in 1987, where she met her two Chinese half-sisters for the first time. In the book, the very similar story of Jing-Mei Woo, who is preparing to go see her two half-sisters in China shortly after her mother's death, provides the narrative structure upon which the other stories are hung. Tan was also inspired by Louise Erdrich's *Love Medicine* (1984) —a multiple-narrator novel that details the experiences of Native Americans in the United States. *The Joy Luck Club* was adapted as a critically acclaimed film in 1993, where Tan served as both co-producer and co-screenwriter. As one of the linked stories in *The Joy Luck Club*, "Rules of the Game" can be found in any edition of Tan's book. The most widely available version is the current paperback edition, published by Ivy Books in 1995.

Author Biography

Tan was born on February 19, 1952, in Oakland, California, two and a half years after her parents emigrated from China. Her father was educated as an engineer in Beijing, but eventually chose to become a Baptist minister. Tan's mother was the daughter of an upper class family in Shanghai, forced to leave three children behind in China while fleeing an unhappy arranged marriage. During Tan's teenage years, she lost both her father and brother to brain tumors.

After the passing of her brother and father, Tan's mother confessed to her that she had two surviving half-sisters who still resided in China. This information would come to be one of many autobiographical elements she would use in her works. Finally receiving the opportunity to meet her sisters in 1987, this became inspiration for the framework of her first novel, *The Joy Luck Club*, published in 1989.

The book received the Commonwealth Club gold award for fiction and the American Library Association's best book for young adults that same year. In 1990, she received the Bay Area Reviewers Award for fiction and was also a finalist for the National Book Award and the National Book Critics Circle Award. The film version of *The Joy Luck Club* premiered in 1993 and became a critically acclaimed film. Tan co-wrote the script and co-produced the film.

In 1991, Tan published her second novel, *The Kitchen God's Wife*, which used two heroines (as opposed to the eight in *The Joy Luck Club)* to continue exploring the generation gap between Chinese-born mothers and their American-born daughters. Other publications by Tan include *The Moon Lady* (1992), *The Chinese Siamese Cat* (1994), *The Hundred Secret Senses* (1995), and *The Bonesetter's Daughter* (2001).

In addition to her writing, Tan has one other interesting "literary" pursuit: she plays the tambourine in a rock band, "The Rock Bottom Remainders," with other famous writers: Stephen King, Matt Groening, Robert Fulghum, and Dave Barry. Tan lives and works in Del Mar, California.

Plot Summary

The Art of Invisible Strength

"Rules of the Game" is one of the interconnected stories in Tan's book, *The Joy Luck Club*. At the beginning of this story, the narrator, Waverly Jong, explains how her mother taught her the art of invisible strength when she was six years old, saying that it is a strategy for winning arguments, respect, and chess games, although she was unaware of the last one at the time she learned the art.

Waverly Place

Waverly describes her home in San Francisco's Chinatown, on a street called Waverly Place. She lives over a Chinese bakery, and as a result, her family's flat always smells good. Although Waverly and her two brothers like to play on the sandlot playground at the end of their alley, they are most fascinated by the alley itself, which contains a number of traditional Chinese businesses like a medicinal herb shop, a fish market, and a Chinese café. The Chinese and American worlds collide on occasion, as when a Caucasian man with a camera takes a picture of Waverly and her friends in front of Hong Sing's, the Chinese café. Waverly's official name is Waverly Place Jong (named after her street), but her family calls her

Meimei, meaning "Little Sister," since she is the youngest and the only daughter.

The Chess Set

When Waverly and her family go to the annual Christmas party at the First Chinese Baptist Church the next year, the children get to pick out gifts that have been donated by another church, which are given out by a Chinese Santa Claus. One little boy gets a globe-shaped coin bank, but he is distressed when he finds only pennies inside. The boy's mother slaps him for his lack of humility, which is a very un-Chinese way to react to a gift. Waverly notes from the other gifts that size does not necessarily equal quality, and when it is her turn, she picks a heavy, compact gift that turns out to be a twelve-pack of Life Savers candies. Her brother Winston gets a model of a World War II submarine, while Vincent, Waverly's other brother, gets a used chess set that is missing a couple of pieces. Although their mother makes a point of declaring in public that the chess set is too nice of a gift, when they get home, she instructs Vincent to throw it out, saying that if it was not good enough for the woman who donated it, then Vincent does not need it either. Vincent does not listen, and he and Winston read the rule book and begin playing chess.

Waverly Begins to Play Chess

Waverly pesters her brothers to let her play the winner, but they do not want her to. Finally, when she offers to use her Life Savers as replacements for the buttons that her brothers are using in place of the missing pieces, they relent and let her play. Waverly does not understand why the rules are the way they are, and asks this, annoying her brothers in the process. Waverly's mother pipes in, talking about American rules, and how when she came over to America, she had to know the rules to get into the country. She tells Waverly that it is better to follow the rules without asking questions, and learn them on your own later. Waverly does this, reading the rule book and even consulting other chess books in the Chinatown library. She learns the strategies of chess, and learns that it is better not to reveal one's knowledge, because chess is a game of secrets where a piece of knowledge unknown to one's opponent can provide the advantage necessary to win the game.

Waverly becomes so good at chess that her brothers get tired of losing to her, and move on to their next diversion—playing cowboys. In the meantime, Waverly sees a bunch of old men playing chess in the park, and approaches one to see if he wants to play chess with her. The man, Lau Po, plays many games with Waverly over the next several weeks, helping her to develop new tactics and at the same time, teaching her the mystical names of these strategies. He also teaches her chess etiquette. Waverly starts to gather a crowd on weekends, and one man encourages Waverly and her mother to have Waverly compete in chess tournaments. Waverly is unsure, and tells her mother that she does not want to shame her family by losing. Her mother replies that this is not shame, shame is doing something stupid like falling down when you have not been pushed.

Chess Tournaments

In her first chess tournament, Waverly earns a trophy. Her first opponent is a fifteen-year-old boy from Oakland. While she plays, she gets into the zone, letting her surroundings drop away and concentrating only on the chess board and pieces, which seem to be full of life in her mind. This ability to use the invisible strength that her mother had taught her leads to many more tournaments, and she wins every time. After winning a regional tournament, she picks up sponsorships from three businesses for her national tournaments, and by the time she turns nine, Waverly is a national chess champion.

The Argument

Waverly's life becomes centered around chess, which is all she concentrates on besides school. Although her parents make concessions for Waverly's chess practice—such as giving her a room separate from her brothers and allowing her to leave the table before she's finished eating—the relationship between Waverly and her mother is strained, as her mother insists on peering over her shoulder and making critical noises at every move. The ultimate falling out between mother and daughter occurs during an otherwise normal trip to the store that Waverly takes with her mother one non-tournament weekend.

Waverly's mother insists on pointing her daughter out to passers-by. This embarrasses Waverly, and she tells her mother that, if she wants to brag, she should learn to play chess herself. Her mother is shocked and angry, and Waverly becomes frightened and runs away. Waverly returns home later that evening, at which time Waverly's mother tells Waverly that she is no longer concerned with her daughter. Waverly goes to her room, where she envisions an imaginary chessboard, upon which her white pieces are annihilated by her mother's black pieces.

Characters

A Caucasian Man

Earlier in her childhood, a caucasian man poses Waverly and her friends in front of Hong Sing's Chinese café and then takes their picture.

The Fifteen-Year-Old Boy

In Waverly's first chess tournament, she squares off against a fifteen-year-old boy, who wrinkles his nose at her, obviously not impressed by the eight-year-old.

Bobby Fischer

In the story, Bobby Fischer—who in real life is the youngest chess player ever to be awarded the rank of grand master—shows up in a *Life* article next to Waverly Jong's picture, where he is quoted as saying that there will never be a woman grand master.

Lindo Jong

Lindo Jong, Waverly's mother, teaches her daughter and two sons the art of invisible strength, a number of Chinese wisdoms that can be used when developing strategies for winning arguments, respect, and in Waverly's case, the game of chess. Lindo's English is stilted, and she speaks in short, clipped phrases, which Waverly often views as criticism, especially when her mother is hanging over her shoulder giving advice while she practices her chess games. Lindo is very vigilant over what her children say and do, and is a very proud woman who generally exhibits proper Chinese humility in public. A good example is when her son, Vincent, receives a used and broken chess set at the church Christmas party. She acts gracious in public, but when they get home, she tells Vincent to throw the game out, saying that they do not need other people's trash. Vincent does not listen, and when he is reading the chess rulebook, Lindo speaks up, saying that the rules of chess are just another set of American rules, and that she, too, had to learn American rules before they would let her into the country.

She cautions Waverly that it is not wise to ask why a rule is the way it is—instead, it is better to find out for yourself. This piece of advice helps Waverly to develop her chess technique. Lindo is supportive of Waverly's chess playing, watching from the crowd when Waverly plays in the park on weekends. At these times, she is properly humble according to Chinese custom, saying that Waverly's winning is just luck. However, after Waverly starts to win more tournaments and becomes a national chess champion, Lindo starts to show Waverly off to others in public. Waverly is embarrassed by her mother's behavior and says so one day, which sparks an argument. Waverly runs away, and when she returns home later that evening, Lindo tells her she is no longer a concern of hers. Waverly goes to her room and tries to figure out what to do next.

Vincent Jong

Vincent Jong, one of Waverly's two older brothers, introduces her to the game of chess. At the annual church Christmas party, he receives a used chess set that is missing a couple of pieces. When Waverly offers to give him Life Savers to use in place of the missing chess pieces, Vincent allows her to play with him and Winston, Waverly's other brother. Vincent tries to explain the rules of the game to Waverly, but she is confused at first. Like Winston, Vincent tires of playing chess after Waverly repeatedly beats him at the game, and the two brothers start to play cowboys instead, prompting Waverly to seek out Lau Po as a chess opponent.

Waverly Place Jong

Waverly Place Jong, the narrator and protagonist of the story, uses her mother's art of "invisible strength" to achieve national fame as a chess champion. The novel begins with Jong recalling when she was six years old and her mother taught her the art of invisible strength—a collection of Chinese wisdoms that can be adapted to many life situations and, in the case of the Jongs, help them to rise above their circumstances. Waverly is fascinated by the Chinatown alley in which she lives, where she and her brothers, Vincent and Winston, peer into Chinese shops like Li's medicinal herb store or Hong Sing's, a Chinese café. Waverly's mother has named her after the street they live on, Waverly Place—also a formal name for official American documents. However, Lindo and the rest of the family usually call Waverly "Meimei," meaning "Little Sister," because she is the youngest child and the only daughter.

When her brother, Vincent, gets a chess set at their church Christmas party, Waverly is the one who turns out to be most adept at the game. After researching the rules of the game and learning the basic moves, she is able to beat both of her brothers, who promptly stop playing the game with her. Instead, Waverly plays with Lau Po, an old man in the park who teaches her chess technique and etiquette. An observer at one of these casual matches encourages Waverly's mom to enter her in a chess tournament, and Waverly takes home a trophy. She moves on to regional, and then national tournaments, picking up sponsorships from local businesses to support her efforts.

Although her mother supports her, Waverly feels pressured, as when her mother tells Waverly after her first win that she should concentrate on losing less pieces. Still, Waverly's mother is supportive of her daughter's chess playing, and even exempts her from certain chores or family customs when she is practicing her chess games. However, mother and daughter get in an argument when Waverly draws attention to the fact that her mother is using her to show off to others. Waverly runs away, and when she returns home later that evening, Waverly's mother tells her that she is no longer a concern of hers. Waverly retires to her bedroom, where she imagines her mother destroying her in a game of chess, and tries to figure out her next move.

Winston Jong

Winston is one of Waverly's two older brothers, who gets a model of a World War II submarine at the annual church Christmas party. Winston plays chess against his brother Vincent and Waverly, until Waverly starts to beat them both repeatedly and the brothers lose interest in chess, turning to playing cowboys instead.

Lau Po

Lau Po is the old man in the park whom Waverly challenges to a game of chess; one game leads to several weeks' worth of games, during which Lau Po helps Waverly expand her knowledge of chess strategies and etiquette. Waverly says that Lau Po is what the man allows her to call him, so it is unclear whether this is the man's real name or a nickname.

Media Adaptations

- *The Joy Luck Club* was released as an audio book in December 1989. It was published by Dove Books and read by the author. This media adaptation is an abridged version of the book.

- Director Wayne Wang's *The Joy Luck Club* was released as a film in September 1993 by Hollywood Pictures and starred Vu Mai as the young Waverly, Tamlyn Tomita as the older Waverly, and Tsai Chin as Lindo Jong. The screenplay was adapted by Tan herself with Ronald Bass, and Wayne Wang directed. The movie is available on VHS from Hollywood Pictures Home Video.

Li

Li is the old man who owns a medicinal herb shop in the alley where Waverly Jong plays; she and her brothers are fascinated by the cures that Li provides to his customers.

A Man

A man who watched Waverly play chess in the park encourages her mother to let Waverly play in local chess tournaments.

Meimei

See Waverly Place Jong

An Old Woman

When Waverly turns to run away from her mother after they have a fight, she bumps into an old woman, knocking her and her bag of groceries to the ground. As Waverly's mother helps the old woman up, Waverly runs away. Both women scream at the fleeing girl.

Waverly's Father

Although it is not mentioned in this story, other stories in *The Joy Luck Club* note how this is Lindo Jong's second husband, although he is Waverly's birth father. Waverly's father works during the days and so is not around as much as her mother, who is the strongest influence in her life.

Waverly's Mother

See Lindo Jong

Chinese Americans

Most of the characters in "Rules of the Game" are Chinese Americans, and much of the conflict is derived from Waverly's attempt to navigate both the traditional Chinese culture and the divergent melding culture of Chineses Americans. When she is younger, Waverly is mainly in touch with her Chinese side. She lives over a small Chinese bakery in Chinatown, where "by daybreak, our flat was heavy with the odor of fried sesame balls and sweet curried chicken crescents." Outside her home, Waverly is drawn to other Chinese establishments, like the Ping Yuen Fish Market, with its "doomed fish and turtles" and a sign that informs tourists, "Within this store, is all for food, not for pet." Most importantly, however, is the Chinese philosophy that Waverly's mother teaches her when she is six years old. "The art of invisible strength," a collection of Chinese "daily truths," is a "strategy for winning arguments [and] respect from others."

As she gets older, however, Waverly becomes more influenced by American culture, becoming so overjoyed when she receives "a twelve-pack of Life Savers" at her church's annual Christmas party that she spends "the rest of the party arranging and rearranging the candy tubes in the order of my favorites." The biggest American influence on

Waverly is the chess set her brother, Vincent, receives as a gift at the same Christmas party. Waverly learns to play chess on her brother's board, quickly becoming very good at the American game, but relying on her Chinese "invisible strength" to do so: "A light wind began blowing past my ears. It whispered secrets only I could hear.... I saw a clear path, the traps to avoid."

Throughout Waverly's short career as a chess player, both she and her mother exhibit distinctly Chinese and American behaviors. When Waverly first starts playing chess, her mother sits "proudly on the bench, telling my admirers with proper Chinese humility, 'Is Luck.'" However, later, when Waverly is becoming a famous chess player, her mother teaches her to sit "in the manner my mother had shown me for posing for the press." This combination of Chinese humility and American publicity is one of many cross-cultural occurrences in the story.

Mothers and Daughters

Waverly's relationship with her mother in the beginning of the story is good, but it deteriorates over time as Waverly becomes more Americanized. When Waverly is six years old, she throws a fit when her mother tells her not to beg for the candy that she wants. "Wise guy, he not go against wind," says her mother, imparting her first lesson on the art of invisible strength to Waverly, who learns to be patient and happily receives candy on the next shopping trip.

Waverly's mother is supportive of her daughter's chess playing, and goes with Waverly to her tournaments. At Waverly's first tournament, "my mother sat with me in the front row as I waited for my turn." Waverly's mother shows her affection for her daughter right before Waverly starts to play. "My mother unwrapped something in her lap. It was her *chang*, a small tablet of red jade which held the sun's fire. 'Is luck,' she whispered, and tucked it into my dress pocket." Waverly's mother is proud of her daughter, but when she tells Waverly at home that she should concentrate on losing less pieces during the game—"Next time win more, lose less."—Waverly is annoyed. However, she notes that "I couldn't say anything," since Waverly follows her mother's advice in the next tournament and does in fact win the match while losing fewer pieces. Waverly's mother also hovers over her daughter's shoulder during practices at home. Says Waverly, "I think she thought of herself as my protective ally. Her lips would be sealed tight, and after each move I made, a soft 'Hmmmmph' would escape from her nose." When Waverly tells her mother that this bugs her, it hurts her mother, who makes the same noise from across the room, although this time it comes "out of her tight throat."

The final insult by Waverly comes after her mother is telling people about Waverly's chess abilities in public. Waverly tells her mother off in public, saying that "I wish you wouldn't do that, telling everybody I'm your daughter." Waverly's mother is shocked and hurt at this statement, especially when she pushes Waverly to explain what she means, and Waverly says, "Why do you have to use me to show off? If you want to show off, then why do not you learn to play chess?" From this point until the end of the story, relations between Waverly and her mother are strained.

Topics for Further Study

- The story takes place in San Francisco's Chinatown, an Asian community, and one of the many culturally diverse areas in the United States. Research the closest large city to your area and see if you can find at least three distinct cultural communities within that city's region. How do these communities differ from your own? In what ways are they the same?

- Although the advent of communism in China in 1949 is not discussed at length in the story, the larger work, *The Joy Luck Club*, is based upon the experiences of four Chinese women who have fled communism and emigrated to the United States, as many did at the time. Research this period of terror and uncertainty in China and write a journal entry from the perspective of a man who is fleeing China at the same time. How would this man's experiences be different from the women's?

- Waverly Jong's main talent in this story is playing chess. Research the history of the game, including finding out where and when it originated and when it began being played in the United States.

- Chess sets come in all shapes and sizes, from cheap, mass-produced plastic sets to one-of-a-kind sets crafted out of marble or other exotic materials. Limited-edition chess sets often follow a theme, which can be something historical such as World War II or something as pop cultural as the characters of a television show. Keeping the story's major themes and background history in mind, design a sample chess set—

using any medium you would like to present your ideas, such as drawing, painting, or sculpture.

Poverty

Waverly and her family do not have a lot of money, but as she notes in the beginning of the story, "Like most of the other Chinese children who played in the back alleys of restaurants and curio shops, I didn't think we were poor." Tan includes some examples that demonstrate the family's poverty, however, as when Waverly is one of many Chinese children who receive donated gifts at their church: "The missionary ladies had put together a Santa bag of gifts donated by members of another church." When Waverly's brother, Vincent, receives a used chess set from this Christmas party, his mother is too proud to accept a used gift, and tells Vincent to get rid of it. Vincent does not want to, even after he finds out that it is "missing a black pawn and a white knight." Vincent and Waverly do not have money to buy replacement pieces, so they improvise, as Waverly notes: "Vincent at first refused to let me play, but when I offered my Life Savers as replacements for the buttons that filled in for the missing pieces, he relented."

Chess

The game of chess is explored in two distinct

ways in the story. The first way is in a rules sense, where Waverly discusses the actual strategies of the game, such as "opening moves and why it is important to control the center early on," "the middle game," and "why it is essential in the endgame to have foresight." These are classic chess strategies, and read almost like an instruction manual.

However, the game of chess also takes on a mythical quality reminiscent of Waverly's Chinese heritage. Says Waverly, "That is the power of chess. It is a game of secrets in which one must show and never tell." Waverly explores this idea more when she starts playing chess with Lau Po, the Chinese man who helps her improve her technique. "I added new secrets. Lau Po gave me the names. The Double Attack from the East and West Shores. Throwing Stones on the Drowning Man. The Sudden Meeting of the Clan." All of these names are Chinese in flavor, and when used along with Waverly's invisible strength, where Waverly seems to actually hear the right moves in the wind, they take on a mythical quality.

This mythical feeling reaches its height after Waverly has gotten angry with her mother on a public street. Back home, Waverly envisions playing an imaginary chess game against her mother: "In my head, I saw a chessboard with sixty-four black and white squares. Opposite me was my opponent, two angry black slits. She wore a triumphant smile." In this struggle, Waverly becomes the loser, and her "white pieces screamed as they scurried and fell off the board one by one."

Style

Point of View

As with the other stories in *The Joy Luck Club*, "Rules of the Game" is narrated from the perspective of one of the main characters. In this case, Waverly Jong gives her point of view about the part of her childhood where she became a chess champion. Waverly narrates the story from her childhood perspective, and does not refer to anything that happened to her as an adult as a result of the events in the story, or give her adult perspective about the events—as some adult narrators do when talking about their childhoods.

Waverly recalls exactly how she felt at each stage of the story. In the beginning, when she is more in touch with her Chinese heritage, she notes that her "bowl was always full," and that her meals began "with a soup full of mysterious things that I didn't want to know the names of." However, after she begins to take an interest in chess, she recalls how "the chessmen were more powerful than old Li's magic herbs that cured ancestral curses," referencing one of the other mysteries that enraptured her as a child. And when Waverly explains the transformation she goes through after she loses the imaginary chess game with her mother. Waverly says, "I rose up into the air and flew out the window. Higher and higher.... up toward the night sky until everything disappeared and I was alone." By telling the reader exactly how she felt at the various points in her childhood and not tainting the narrative with her adult perspective, Waverly's child point of view walks the reader through her transformation, step by step, which leads to a more powerful ending.

Setting

For many of Tan's readers, Chinese culture is unfamiliar, so the vivid descriptions of everyday life in San Francisco's Chinatown help to educate readers at the same time as it entertains. In the medicinal herb store, Waverly and her brothers watch "old Li dole out onto a stiff sheet of white paper the right amount of insect shells, saffron-colored seeds, and pungent leaves for his ailing customers." This description evokes some strong images in the reader's mind, while giving some background information on the traditional Chinese belief in holistic healing. The same is true with the description of Ping Yuen Fish Market, where "the butchers with their bloodstained white smocks deftly gutted the fish while customers cried out their orders," and where Waverly and her brothers "inspect the crates of live frogs and crabs which we were warned not to poke, boxes of dried cuttlefish, and row upon row of iced prawns, squid, and slippery fish." These candid descriptions highlight the fact that seafood is one of the staples of the Chinese diet. They also show how, in Chinese culture, food is prepared fresh for customers, with no attempt to hide the sometimes messy method of preparation. This is a stark contrast to the sterile environments found in most American butcher shops or fish markets, where much of the preparation is done out of the customer's sight.

Language

Tan's accurate portrayal of Chinese Americans, including the stilted English that many Chinese-born Americans speak, was one of the reasons why *The Joy Luck Club* became such a popular and critical success. In "Rules of the Game," this stilted English is demonstrated through Waverly's mother. Waverly remembers one of her mother's stories, in which a girl runs out into the street and gets crushed by a car. "Was smash flat," says Waverly's mother. This short sentence, which is a truncated version of the grammatically correct phrase, "She was smashed flat," is still understandable. Likewise, when Waverly asks her mother about Chinese torture, her mother asks "Who say this word?" instead of "Who said this word?" In this case, only one word is grammatically incorrect. However, by changing this one word, "said" to "say," the feeling of the phrase changes, and gives it the traditional Chinese character that Tan wanted to demonstrate in Waverly's mother. This pattern is repeated throughout the story, and shows up in longer sections of dialogue with Waverly's mother, such as when Waverly wins her chess match while losing less of her pieces. Waverly's mother says, "Lost eight piece this time.

Last time was eleven. What I tell you? Better off lose less!"

Personification

The story relies on the technique of personification—attributing human qualities to inanimate objects—to give it more life. Tan personifies many items in the story, most notably after Waverly begins to play chess. When Waverly plays in her first tournament, her invisible strength manifests itself as a wind that "whispered secrets only I could hear." In real life, a wind can't whisper, only humans can. However, by describing the wind in this way, it becomes more animated and helps to reinforce the idea of Waverly's magical ability to see things differently from others. Likewise, in the same chess match, Waverly says that "The knight came forward ready for the sacrifice." Chess pieces can't move of their own power, and certainly do not commit hari kari. However, by using this kind of elaborate language, it paints a vivid picture in the reader's mind. Waverly could have said that she is moving her knight in a position where he will be taken by her opponent, but by personifying the knight, she once again helps to reinforce the idea that her invisible strength is a magical ability.

In addition to personifying Waverly's invisible strength and her chess playing, Tan uses personification in other ways, such as expressing Waverly's mood. Near the end of the story, after Waverly runs away from her mother, her breath comes out "like angry smoke," reflecting Waverly's anger towards her mother. Likewise, when Waverly comes home, she finds her parents at dinner. While waiting for her punishment, Waverly notices the remains of dinner: "a large fish, its fleshy head still connected to bones swimming upstream in vain escape." Waverly is feeling like she needs to escape but, like the fish, knows she has nowhere to run to.

People's Republic of China

On January 21, 1949, China's civil war—
between Communists and Chinese nationalists—
came to an end when Communist forces, led by
Mao Zedong, defeated China's Nationalist
government, which had stopped receiving aid from
the United States. The Chinese president, Chiang
Kai-Shek, resigned, and shortly thereafter, Mao's
forces took over Beijing. During the next several
months, those peasants who didn't support
Communism—like Waverly's mother and the other
mothers in *The Joy Luck Club*, fled mainland China
for American soil, settling in Asian hot spots like
San Francisco's Chinatown. Critic Walter Shear, in
his *Critique* review, references this historical
situation, saying "those millions of Chinese who
were part of the diaspora [migration] of World War
II and the fighting that resulted in the triumph of the
Communists," were unfortunately left without a
home when they were "cut off from the mainland
and after 1949 left to fend for themselves
culturally." Although this is not discussed at length
in the story, "Rules of the Game," Waverly's
mother hints at this when she notes her own
experience trying to emigrate to America when she
says: "Every time people come out from foreign
country, must know rules. You not know, judge say,
Too bad, go back."

However, it would have been difficult for Waverly's mother, or any other Chinese person settling in America, to consider going back to China. On October 1, 1949, seven months after Mao and his Communist forces took over Beijing, Mao announced the formation of the People's Republic of China, in which he would serve as chairman. Mao, who had been a peasant himself, promised a Communist utopia. But when he gave preference to wealthy landowners, and attempted to instill new land reforms, landlords and tenants staged bloody battles. Mao, who had come in only as a chairman for the "people's" republic, turned quickly into a dictator. During his first years as ruler, Mao's reforms plunged China into turmoil and famine, and nobody who had escaped the mainland would willingly choose to go back.

Compare & Contrast

- **1950s:** Chairman Mao Zedong rules as Communist dictator in the People's Republic of China.

   1980s: Chinese students in Beijing's Tiananmen Square stage a pro-democracy demonstration. Hundreds are killed when the Chinese government suppresses the protesters with tear gas, rifle fire, and tanks—which crush protesters.

   Today: China is the only remaining Communist major power in the world.

- **1950s:** Fifteen-year-old American, Bobby Fischer, becomes the world's youngest chess player ever to attain the rank of grand master, making chess history.

  1980s: After two decades of programming computers to play chess, Deep Thought, a computer designed to play chess at the level of the grand masters, is created. At the same time, HiTech, a computer developed at Carnegie Mellon University, defeats a human grand master for the first time.

  Today: Deep Blue, Deep Thought's successor, defeats Russian Garry Kasparov, world chess champion, in one of the biggest upsets in chess history.

- **1950s:** Senator Joseph McCarthy instigates national fear and panic, by claiming that there are many Communist sympathizers living in the United States. Through a series of witch-hunts and trials by the United States Congress House Committee on Un-American Activities, many Chinese Americans, the victims of racial profiling, are put under suspicion, interrogated, and otherwise harassed.

1980s: Many multicultural authors —like Tan, Louise Erdrich, and Oscar Hijuelos—who have been assimilated into modern American culture, try to reconcile their two cultures through their fiction. Many of these books are received well by American readers, and the field of multicultural literature expands.

Today: Wen Ho Lee, a Chinese-American scientist at the Los Alamos National Laboratory, is investigated to determine whether or not he leaked nuclear secrets to China. Many Asian Americans claim they are being discriminated against as a result of this negative exposure.

- **1950s:** Following World War II, the relaxing of anti-Chinese immigration laws, and the advent of Communist rule in China, many Chinese settle in the United States, in ethnic enclaves like San Francisco's Chinatown.

1980s: In films like *Gremlins, Big Trouble in Little China*, and *The Golden Child*, San Francisco's Chinatown is depicted as a mystical place, often for humorous effect.

Today: Due in large part to the American-released films of popular actors like Hong Kong's Jackie Chan and Chow Yun Fat, other Asian enclaves in America are depicted. However, in these films, pure martial arts and other forms of action often replace Chinese mysticism.

McCarthyism

Mao's Communist victory in China added to the United States's fear of the spread of Communism, which also reigned in the Soviet Union and Eastern Europe. In 1950, a little-known senator, Joseph McCarthy, capitalized on this fear when he instigated a national inquiry, attempting to root out potential Communist sympathizers. McCarthy, who used many props but provided very little evidence, turned Americans against themselves, and as a result many innocent people—including hordes of Chinese Americans—were persecuted or harassed. As Martin Gilbert notes in his *A History of the Twentieth Century*, "It was a witch-hunt of the most virulent sort, nationwide and relentless." Although "Rules of the Game" takes place in the late 1950s, long after McCarthy had been censured for his actions, Americans were still anxious about the possibility of Communists living in their area. This is hinted at in the story when Waverly goes to the Christmas party, and the Chinese Santa Claus "solemnly asked if I had been a very, very good girl this year and did I believe in Jesus Christ and obey my parents." Waverly, who was born in 1951, and who grew up in the pro-religion and anti-Communist atmosphere of the 1950s, "knew the only answer to that. I nodded back with equal solemnity."

Bobby Fischer

Bobby Fischer was a chess prodigy, like Waverly Jong in "Rules of the Game." Fischer learned how to play chess when he was only six years old, became the world's youngest person to reach the rank of grand master (at age fifteen in 1958), and dropped out of school at sixteen to play chess full-time. Fischer became a legend in the chess world, as much for his attitude as for his masterful playing. Fischer's skill reached its peak in 1972, when he defeated Soviet player and world champion, Boris Spassky, to become the first American player to win the world Chess Champion of the World title. Three years later, however, Fischer refused to defend his title against another Soviet opponent, Anatolly Karpov, an act that prompted the International Chess Federation to strip Fischer of his title and give it to Karpov by default. Fischer didn't return to the competitive chess scene until almost two decades later, when he defeated Spassky again in a rematch.

Increase in Asian-American Population

It was not until the 1940s, when Japan became the enemy during World War II, that Congress began to repeal the Chinese immigration restriction laws that had been put in place in the late nineteenth and early twentieth centuries. As the laws were changed, more Chinese Americans were allowed to attend American universities and enter professional fields like medicine, corporate business, and engineering, giving them the means to move out of urban areas like San Francisco's Chinatown and into suburbs. In 1990, a year after Tan wrote *The Joy Luck Club*, the number of Asians living in the United States had increased from about 875,000 in 1960 to about seven million. Of these, more than 1.6 million were of Chinese descent, and more than 700,000 Chinese Americans lived in California—many in San Francisco's Chinatown, which even today continues to host one of the world's largest Chinese communities outside of Asia.

Critical Overview

Tan's first novel, *The Joy Luck Club*, which includes Waverly Jong's childhood story in "Rules of the Game," was a smash success with both popular and critical readers. In her review in the *The Nation*, Valerie Miner called the book "a stunningly auspicious debut," and called Tan "a gifted storyteller who reaches across cultures and generations." Orville Schell of *The New York Times Review of Books* called it "a jewel of a book," while Scarlet Cheng, in *Belles Lett res*, commended it for its "clarity of voice and lucidity of vision."

Of course, it is rare to find a book that is wholly and universally loved by all, and *The Joy Luck Club* is no exception. The majority of the negative criticism has been about the book's structure. As David Gates noted in his *Newsweek* review, "Waverly is just one of eight main characters—four Chinese-born mothers and their American-born daughters—in *The Joy Luck Club.*" In total, the book contains sixteen individual stories from these characters. Said Charlotte Painter, in the *San Francisco Review of Books*, "The book holds technical difficulties Tan has not overcome. The voices, in unrelieved first person, resemble one another too closely." As Gates said, "such an ambitious narrative scheme would be a handful for any writer; inevitably the voices sound alike." And in *Melus*, Ben Xu characterized the book as "neither a novel nor a group of short stories. It consists of isolated acts and events, which remain scattered and disbanded."

To Gates, however, "Tan is so gifted that none of this matters much." Likewise, in the *Christian Science Monitor*, Merle Rubin called each story "a gem, complete in itself," and said that "In Tan's hands, these linked stories—diverse as they are—fit almost magically into a powerfully coherent novel."

Several critics remarked on the themes inherent in all of the stories, most notably the experience of Chinese Americans. In fact, as Dorothy Wang noted of Tan after an interview with the author, "her insights into the complexities of being a hyphenated American, connected by blood and bonds to another culture and country, have found a much wider audience than Tan had ever imagined." Schell cited *The Joy Luck Club* as part of "a new genre of American fiction," which began with the works of writers like Maxine Hong Kingston. Walter Shear was another critic who noted the similarity of Tan's works to Hong Kingston's, saying in his review in *Critique* that the two authors' abilities "to render the experience of a culture through vividly dramatic individual narratives," is helping to develop a "tradition of Chinese-American women's writing." In *The Women's Review of Books*, Helen Yglesias praised Tan for veering away from traditional stereotypes of Chinese women, saying that "there isn't a single Chinese laundry ... and no Dragon Ladies. Tan rescued the Chinese-American woman from numbing distortion in *The Joy Luck Club*."

Critics have also noted the second major theme in the book, the relationships between mothers and daughters. In her review in *Quill and Quire*, Denise Chong called the stories "moving and powerful," saying that they "share the irony, pain, and sorrow of the imperfect ways in which mothers and daughters love each other." Other critics, like Miner, noted Tan's "remarkable ear for dialogue and dialect," saying that the author represented both "the choppy English of the mothers and the sloppy California vernacular of the daughters with sensitive authenticity."

In addition to the novel as a whole, some critics have remarked upon the individual stories, such as "Rules of the Game." Gates noted that Tan seemed to take the advice that she put in Waverly Jong's mouth, about withholding knowledge to be used later. Said Gates, "Tan is so cagey it takes a while to discern that fetching little Waverly... has become a disagreeable young woman." And Cheng noted the author's use of "invisible strength," in the story saying that this "fundamental faith in invisible forces pervades traditional Chinese culture."

Perhaps the best praise of all came from Carolyn See, of the *Los Angeles Times Book Review*, who said, "The only negative thing I could ever say about this book is that I'll never again be able to read it for the first time."

What Do I Read Next?

- *Love Medicine*, written by Louise Erdrich and originally published in 1984, was reprinted in 1993 by HarperPerennial Library when the author added five new chapters to the novel. This book is a series of interwoven stories about different generations in a Native American family. In 1985, Amy Tan read this book and was influenced heavily by it when she wrote *The Joy Luck Club*.

- *The Woman Warrior: Memoirs of a Girlhood among Ghosts*, originally published in 1976, is a memoir of a Chinese-American girl growing up in Stockton, California. There are two worlds that the girl lives between, America—the place her parents emigrated to—and China, which the girl hears about in her mother's "talk-stories." Written by Maxine Hong Kingston, the first critically successful Asian-American writer in the United States, the book helped pave the way for Asian-American writers like Amy Tan.

- *How To Think in Chess* was written by Jan Przewoznik and Marek Soszynski and was published in 2001 by Russell Enterprises. This book uses psychological experiments to show how professional chess players really think, how they "see" the chessboard. It then teaches readers to examine their own thought process when playing chess, so that they will be able to discover how they may be limiting their potential.

- *The Bonesetter's Daughter*, by Amy Tan, was published in 2002 by Ballantine Books. This book is about a mother who has been diagnosed with Alzheimer's disease and becomes determined to write a record of her birth and family history, so that she will not forget the details of her life as her memory continues to deteriorate. Her daughter, a ghost writer for self-help books, has little knowledge of her mother's history. The daughter becomes determined to improve the bad relationship she has with her mother and to try to find out who her mother really is before she loses the opportunity forever.

- *The Kitchen God's Wife*, Amy Tan's second novel, was published by Putnam in 1991. The book further explores the generation gap between Chinese-born mothers and their American-born daughters, but, unlike *The Joy Luck Club*, the story is limited to only two heroines.

- *Searching for Bobby Fischer: The Father of a Prodigy Observes the World of Chess* was written by Fred Waitzkin and published in 1993 by Penguin USA. This book is the story of Waitzkin and his son, Josh. It covers the time period from when a six year-old Josh first sits down at a chessboard until he competes for the national championship. Through this journey, father and son must also work through the challenges of their own difficult relationship.

- *The Complete Idiot's Guide to Chess* was written by Patrick Wolff and published in 2001 by Alpha Books.

Wolff, the current United States Chess Champion and International Grandmaster, teaches quick and easy strategies for learning the basics of chess. This book contains essential information on basic openings and endgames, as well as tips on how to read a rival's moves.

Sources

Cheng, Scarlet, "Your Mother Is in Your Bones," in *Belles Lettres*, Vol. 4, No. 4, Summer 1989, p. 12.

Chong, Denise, "Emotional Journeys through East and West," in *Quill and Quire*, Vol. 55, No. 5, May 1989, p. 23.

Gates, David, "A Game of Show Not Tell," in *Newsweek*, Vol. 113, No. 16, April 17, 1989, p. 68–69.

Gilbert, Martin, *A History of the Twentieth Century*, Vol. 3, *1952–1999*, Perennial, 2000, p. 23.

Ling, Amy, "Focus on America: Seeking a Self and a Place," in *Between Worlds: Women Writers of Chinese Ancestry*, Pergamon Press, 1990, pp. 104–57.

Miner, Valerie, "The Daughters' Journeys," in the *Nation*, Vol. 248, No. 16, April 24, 1989, pp. 566–69.

Painter, Charlotte, "In Search of a Voice," in *San Francisco Review of Books*, Summer 1989, pp. 15–17.

Rubin, Merle, "Chinese-American 'Bridge' Club," in *Christian Science Monitor*, Vol. 81, No. 102, April 21, 1989, p. 13.

Schell, Orville, "'Your Mother Is in Your Bones,'" in the *New York Times Book Review*, March 19, 1989, pp. 3, 28.

See, Carolyn, "Drowning in America, Starving for China," in *Los Angeles Times Book Review*, March 12, 1989, pp. 1, 11.

Shear, Walter, "Generational Differences and the Diaspora," in *Critique*, Vol. 34, No. 3, Spring 1993, pp. 193–99.

Wang, Dorothy, Review of *The Joy Luck Club*, in *Newsweek*, Vol. 113, No. 16, April 17, 1989, p. 69.

Xu, Ben, "Memory and the Ethnic Self: Reading Amy Tan's *The Joy Luck Club*," in *MELUS*, Vol. 19, No. 1, Spring 1994, pp. 3–16.

Yglesias, Helen, "The Second Time Around," in *Women's Review of Books*, Vol. VIII, No. 12, September 1991, pp. 1, 3.

Further Reading

Bloom, Harold, *Amy Tan*, Modern Critical Views series, Chelsea House Publications, 2000.

> This book is a great introduction to the current criticism about Tan's works, including her first novel, *The Joy Luck Club*.

Huntley, E. D., *Amy Tan: A Critical Companion*, Greenwood Publishing Group, 1998.

> Author Amy Tan has become well-known for her ability to present her Asian-American stories in an accessible way for many different families. This book is an in-depth study of Tan's first three novels: *The Joy Luck Club, The Kitchen God's Wife*, and *The Hundred Secret Senses*. All aspects of these novels are explored including the characters, narrative strategies, plot development, literary devices, setting, and major themes.

Lohr, Steve, *Go To: The Story of the Math Majors, Bridge Players, Engineers, Chess Wizards, Scientists and Iconoclasts Who Were the Hero Programmers of the Software Revolution*, Basic Books, 2001.

> This book details the strange history

of computer science, a field where chess wizards were one of many kinds of people recruited by companies like IBM, Microsoft, and Apple for their interest in computers and logical skills in programming. It details the life stories of these people, starting in the 1950s at the dawn of the technological revolution, and discusses the little known but important role of women during this time.

Williams, Gareth, *Master Pieces: The Architecture of Chess*, Viking Press, 2000.

This book is a stunning visual exploration of the art and design of the individual pieces contained in a chess set. It includes information on the history, evolution, and symbolism of chess pieces and discusses the craft of creating chess pieces. Finally, it presents full-color illustrations of some of the most beautiful and famous chess sets from all over the world.

CPSIA information can be obtained
at www.ICGtesting.com
Printed in the USA
LVHW022320170323
741893LV00036B/1905

9 781375 387293